CONTENTS

INTRODUCTION

We all know that yelling at our kids is bad. It's something that we shouldn't do, but sometimes it's hard to control ourselves. Yelling can be a reaction to stress, fatigue, or frustration. It can also be a learned behavior - something we picked up from our own parents or other adults in our lives.

This book will teach you why parents should stop yelling at their kids and how you can accomplish it.

It's important to understand the reasons behind our behavior to change it. So, if you're ready to learn how to stop yelling at your kids, this book is for you!

This parenting book to stop yelling at your kids will cover many topics, including:

- Why Yelling at your Kids is Bad
- Why Parents Yell and What it Accomplishes
- The Effects of Yelling on Kids
- Creative Ways to Get Your Kids to Listen without Yelling
- How to Forgive Yourself after Yelling at Little One

BENEFITS FROM READING THIS BOOK

Yelling is a common problem among parents, but it's not the only way to discipline your little one. In fact, many parenting books, like this one can be extremely helpful in teaching you how to effectively discipline your children without yelling.

Some benefits from reading this book to help you stop yelling include:

1) You'll learn alternative methods of discipline that don't involve yelling
2) You'll understand why parents yell and what it accomplishes
3) You'll learn about the myths surrounding yelling at kids
4) You'll understand the science behind why yelling is harmful
5) You'll get creative ideas for getting your kids to listen without yelling
6) You'll learn how to forgive yourself for yelling
7) You'll take away actionable steps that will help you stop yelling

If you're ready to learn how to stop yelling at your kids, this book is for you!

WHY PARENTS YELL AND WHAT IT ACCOMPLISHES

Before we dive into how to stop yelling, let's explore why parents yell in the first place. There are many reasons why parents might resort to yelling, but some common ones include:

1) Feeling overwhelmed or stressed

You may be more likely to yell if you're feeling overwhelmed or stressed. This is because yelling can be a way to release pent-up frustration.

2) Lack of sleep

If you're running on empty, you may be more likely to yell when your kids don't listen. This is because fatigue can make it difficult to control your emotions.

3) Having unrealistic expectations

If you have unrealistic expectations for your children, you may be more likely to yell when they don't meet them. This is because you may feel like they're not meeting your expectations.

4) Not knowing how to discipline effectively

If you're not sure how to discipline your children effectively, you may resort to yelling. This is because you may not know what else to do.

5) Reacting in the moment without thinking

In the heat of the moment, it can be easy to lash out and yell. This is because you may not be thinking clearly when you're angry or frustrated.

While there are many reasons why parents might yell at their kids, it's important to understand that yelling is not an effective form of discipline. In fact, research has shown that yelling can be harmful to both children and parents.

Yelling might seem like an effective way to discipline your child in the moment, but it doesn't accomplish anything long-term. In fact, yelling can be harmful to both you and your child.

Some of the ways that yelling can be harmful include:

1)   Yelling can damage your relationship with your child
2)   Yelling can lead to increased misbehavior
3)   Yelling can make your child feel insecure, anxious, or scared
4)   Yelling can make you feel guilty and stressed

If you're struggling with yelling at your kids, it's important to understand the reasons why you're doing it. Once you know the reasons, you can start to work on finding alternative methods of discipline.

In this book I cover many alternatives, but before we get into it, let's look at some myths surrounding yelling at your kids.

5 MYTHS ABOUT YELLING AT YOUR KIDS THAT EVERY PARENT SHOULD KNOW

There are many myths surrounding yelling at kids. Some parents believe that yelling is necessary, while others think that it's always harmful. However, the truth is somewhere in between.

Here are 5 myths about yelling at your kids that every parent should know:

Myth #1: Yelling is the only way to get my child's attention

This is a myth because there are many other ways to get your child's attention. You can try using a calm voice, making eye contact, or even calling your child by name.

Myth #2: Yelling is an effective way to discipline my child

This is a myth because yelling is not an effective way to discipline your child. In fact, it can lead to increased misbehavior.

Myth #3: Yelling is the only way I can get my point across

This is a myth because there are many other ways to communicate with your child. You can try using positive reinforcement, providing explanations, or using logical consequences.

Myth #4: Yelling is only harmful if it's done in anger

This is a myth because yelling can be harmful even if it's not done in anger. Yelling can damage your relationship with your child, lead to increased misbehavior, and cause psychological harm.

Myth #5: I can't help but yell at my child

This is a myth because it's possible to stop yelling at your child. If you're struggling with yelling, there are many resources that can help, including parenting books like this one, counselors, and support groups.

Let's have a look at why yelling excessively can be harmful to your child.

THE SCIENCE BEHIND WHY YELLING IS HARMFUL

Yelling is harmful because it causes stress. When you yell at your child, their body releases the stress hormone cortisol. This hormone can lead to physical and emotional problems, like headaches, stomachaches, anxiety, and depression.

In addition to causing stress, yelling can also damage your relationship with your child. Yelling creates an environment of fear, which can make your child feel insecure, anxious, and scared.

If you want to stop yelling at your kids, it's important to understand the science behind why it's harmful. Once you know the reasons why yelling is harmful, you can start to find alternative methods of discipline.

Following are a few alternatives to yelling. All of them may not work for you or every situation, but I'm sure you'll find a few that does!

20 CREATIVE WAYS TO GET YOUR KIDS TO LISTEN WITHOUT YELLING

1) Use a Calm Voice

We've all been there. Your kid is being disobedient or just downright frustrating and you find yourself yelling at them in a last-ditch effort to get them to listen. But yelling can often have the opposite effect, making your kid tune you out or even act out more.

How can you get your kid to listen without resorting to raising your voice? Try using a calm voice instead. It may take some practice, but it's worth it when you see your child start responding better.

Why does using a calm voice to get your kid to listen work?

Kids learn best from example - if you want them to be calm, they need to see you being calm.

Calm voices are more likely to be heard and obeyed than angry ones. A calm voice will help your child feel safe and secure

It teaches them how to handle their emotions in a healthy way. Yelling is mostly unnecessary - a calm voice will usually get the same results.

It's also exhausting for both you and your child. Yelling teaches kids that it's okay to yell when they're upset or angry.

Children learn best through positive reinforcement - yelling will only teach them that they need to be afraid of you. Also, a calm voice will help you stay in control during a stressful situation.

Ways to get your kid to listen by using a calm voice:

- Lower your tone and use a calm voice to get your kid's attention
- Make sure your words are clear and concise - no yelling or speaking in a rushed manner
- Use short, simple sentences that are easy for kids to understand
- Also, be consistent with your commands - always use the same voice and tone when asking your kid to do something

The next time you feel yourself getting frustrated with your child, take a deep breath and try using a calm voice. It may take some practice, but eventually your child will learn to associate that calm voice with positive behavior.

And remember, always praise your child for good behavior – even if it's just taking the trash out on their own! Using a calm voice is a very effective tools in any parent's toolbox.

2) Make Eye Contact

So, your kid is pulling on your last nerve, and you feel like you're about to explode. You've tried yelling, you've tried talking calmly, but nothing seems to be working.

Here's a little secret: the key to getting kids to listen is making eye contact. When they see that you're serious and that you're paying attention, they'll start to take what you have to say more seriously too.

Next time your child is testing your patience, try staring them in the eyes and see what happens. Chances are, they'll back down pretty quickly.

Some reasons why making eye contact is important to get your kid to listen are:

- Eye contact is a form of communication that shows you're paying attention and that you care
- Eye contact is a sign of respect - it shows your child that you value their opinion and want to hear what they have to say
- It teaches kids how to handle difficult conversations in a healthy way
- Yelling can damage the relationship between parent and child, while eye contact builds it up

Eye contact is key when it comes to effective communication with children. It shows them that you're paying attention and that you value what they have to say. When kids feel heard, they're more likely to listen without having to yell.

Next time your child is giving you attitude, try using a calm voice and making eye contact – it just might be the ticket to getting them to finally behave.

3) Call Your Child by Name

I don't know about you, but when my kids are being particularly willful, the first thing that goes through my head is yelling. I'm not proud of it, but sometimes it's just so darn tempting to let loose with a good old-fashioned parental scolding.

And, according to recent studies, apparently, I'm not alone - almost half of all parents admit to regularly yelling at their kids.

But what if there was another way? A better way? A way that could get your kid to listen without raising your voice?

Try calling them by name. It sounds simple (and maybe even a little cheesy), but it really works!

Some reasons why this is effective to get your kid to listen are that when you call your child by name, they know that you're talking to them specifically and that they need to listen.

It's a way to show them that you're paying attention to them and what they're doing. Calling their name gets their attention faster than just yelling at them or using a general term like "kids".

Calling your child by name establishes a sense of authority and respect between you and your child. It makes it easier for them to follow directions because they know who is giving them the instruction.

It teaches them their name is important and they should listen when it's called out. You set the tone for discipline - if you start off by calling their name, they know that you mean business.

It also helps them learn how to focus and pay attention.

How to use this effectively:

- Start with a firm voice and use your child's name
- Make sure you are facing them when you talk to them
- Use a positive tone of voice
- Keep your sentences short and clear
- Be consistent - always use the same rules and expectations
- Reward good behavior with praise or a small treat

The next time you need your child to listen without having to raise your voice, try calling their name. It's a simple strategy that can make a big difference in how well your child responds. And don't forget to use a calm voice – yelling will only aggravate the situation and likely have the opposite effect of what you were hoping for.

4) Use Positive Reinforcement

When it comes to getting your kid to listen, some parents seem to have the knack while others don't. If you're finding yourself in the latter category, don't worry, there's hope.

You can get your kid to listen without yelling by using positive reinforcement. And no, I'm not talking about bribing them with candy or toys. Although that may work in the short-term, it's not a sustainable solution in the long run.

Positive reinforcement means rewarding your child for good behavior with things like praise and hugs. When they know that they're going to receive something positive from you every time they behave well, they'll be much more likely to comply with your requests.

So next time your little one is giving you trouble, try using positive reinforcement instead of yelling – it just might be the key to getting them to finally listen.

Reasons why positive reinforcement works are that positive reinforcement is a powerful tool that can be used to get your child to listen and behave in the way you want them to.

It's important to provide positive reinforcement when your child does something good, as this will encourage them to repeat that behavior in the future. There are many ways to provide positive reinforcement, including verbal praise, rewards, and privileges.

Make sure you stay consistent with these techniques and be patient while your child adjusts to them. Enjoy watching your child blossom into a happy and well-behaved individual by using positive reinforcement!

To use positive reinforcement effectively:

- Start with a positive statement
- Follow up with a clear explanation of what you want your child to do
- Give feedback that is specific and immediate

- Use descriptive words to reinforce good behavior
- Reward your child immediately after they have followed your instructions
- Keep instructions short and simple

By using positive reinforcement, you can help your child listen without having to raise your voice. Remain calm and consistent in your approach and be sure to praise good behavior. Soon enough, you'll find that your child is listening more closely – without all the yelling!

5) Provide Explanations

It's 3 p.m., and you've been trying to get your kid to clean their room for the past hour. You've given them plenty of warnings, but they just don't seem to be listening. What's a parent to do?

Yelling at your child probably won't work but providing explanations may help them understand why it's important to clean their room. In fact, research shows that kids who receive explanations are more likely to comply with requests.

So, the next time you need your child to listen, try providing an explanation instead of yelling. It may just help solve the problem!

Why is giving instructions so effective?

Giving instructions is one of the most effective ways to get your child to listen. Instructions should be clear and concise.

Follow through on what you say - if you tell your child to clean their room, make sure it's clean when they're done. Be patient with your child and praise them when they do follow your instructions.

Don't give too many instructions at once - start with one or two and add more as needed. Use a calm voice when giving instructions - raising your voice will only scare your child and make them less likely to listen.

Tips for giving instructions effectively:

- Use a clear and concise voice when giving instructions
- Make eye contact with your child when speaking
- Avoid using baby talk or excessively raising your voice
- Keep instructions short and to the point
- Repeat yourself if necessary
- Reward your child for following instructions correctly

Giving clear instructions will help your child listen without having to yell. When you need to give a directive, use a calm voice and be specific about what you want your child to do.

If your child doesn't seem to understand what you're asking them to do, take a step back and try explaining it in a different way.

And finally, remember that consistency is key – if you expect your child to follow directions, make sure you always provide clear instructions yourself!

6) Use Logical Consequences

As a parent, you know that sometimes you need to get your kid's attention without yelling. But what do you do when they don't listen? Another strategy is to use logical consequences. By taking away something your child wants as a punishment for their bad behavior, you can encourage them to behave better in the future.

Using logical consequences works because logical consequences are fair - they happen because of the child's own actions, not because someone is mad at them. They're effective because kids want to avoid feeling bad or getting in trouble.

Logical consequences are a natural consequence of the child's behavior, so kids learn from them quickly. You need to be consistent when using logical consequences or else your child will become confused and stop listening.

It's important to have a backup plan in case the logical consequence doesn't work - like giving your child a choice between two undesirable outcomes.

Here are some tips for using logical consequences effectively:

- If your child doesn't listen to you, calmly explain why it's important to listen and what will happen if they don't
- If your child continues not to listen, follow through with the logical consequences you outlined
- Praise your child when they do listen and follow directions

- Help them understand why it's important to listen by providing short and simple explanations
- Be consistent with your expectations and punishments
- Keep calm and avoid getting angry - this will only make things worse

When you give a command, be sure to follow through with a logical consequence. This will help your child learn that listening is important and will reduce the number of times you have to yell.

Use a calm voice when delivering consequences so that your child knows you are serious and still in control. Yelling only serves to scare and confuse children, making it harder for them to understand what they did wrong.

Following through with logical consequences shows your child that you are serious about teaching them right from wrong without having to raise your voice.

7) Give Warnings

Do you ever feel like you're stuck in a never-ending battle with your kids, where no matter what you say or do, they just refuse to listen? It can be incredibly frustrating when all you want is for them to cooperate, and they just won't. But don't worry – there are ways to get your kids to listen without having to resort to yelling. Another way is by giving warnings.

Some reasons that this is an effective tool are that giving your child a warning before you discipline them makes it more likely that they will listen and learn from their mistake. Warnings show your child that you care about them and want them to stay safe.

A warning gives your child a chance to correct their behavior before they get in trouble. It teaches your child to take responsibility for their actions.

Warnings help prevent power struggles between you and your child. They can be used as a teaching tool to help your child understand the relationship between cause and effect.

Tips to keep your warnings effective:

- Establish yourself as the authority figure in your child's life
- Use a clear and consistent tone of voice when giving warnings
- Make sure your child is paying attention when you're giving them a warning
- Keep warnings short and to the point
- Follow through with consequences if your child doesn't listen
- Reward your child for following your warnings

Giving a warning before punishment is often enough to get your child's attention and help them listen the first-time next time. If you do need to give a punishment, make sure it's logical so your child can understand why they are being punished.

Using these techniques should help reduce the number of times you have to raise your voice or yell at your child.

8) Set Limits

Kids can be frustrating. There's no way to sugarcoat it. They're constantly testing boundaries and pushing the limits, and when you finally reach your breaking point, yelling seems like the only option. But yelling isn't effective - in fact, it usually just makes things worse. So what is another way to get your kid to listen without raising your voice? By setting limits.

Limits are a non-verbal way of communicating what is and isn't acceptable behavior. When kids know what the boundaries are, they're less likely to push them, which means less yelling on your part.

Setting limits are important because establishing limits teaches your child that there are rules in life that need to be followed. Limits help your child learn how to control their impulses and make better decisions.

Setting limits teaches your child about respect - for themselves, others, and property. Limits provide a sense of security and stability for your child during times of change or chaos.

Limits give your child boundaries within which they can explore and experiment safely. Limits also help prevent problems down the road by teaching your child how to behave responsibly.

So how do you go about setting limits for your little one?

- Establish rules and consequences together
- Explain why the rule is important
- Be consistent with your limits
- Give your child some control over their life
- Respond calmly to challenging behavior
- Praise good behavior

The brain is constantly seeking balance or homeostasis. This means that when something in the environment is off-balance, the brain will try to correct it.

For kids, this can mean they are constantly testing limits and boundaries. Setting limits for your child helps them feel safe and secure, which in turn allows them to explore and learn.

Limits also help children understand their place in the world and how they relate to others. When you set clear limits and enforce them consistently, it teaches your child important life skills like self-control, respect for authority, and empathy.

9) Offer Choices

It's no secret that parenting can be tough. But one of the toughest challenges is finding ways to get your kids to listen without yelling.

Another approach that can often help is offering choices. For example, you might say "It's time to get ready for bed. Would you like to take a bath or a shower?"

This approach can work especially well with younger kids who may feel overwhelmed by too many instructions at once.

By giving them choices, you're letting them know that they have some control over what happens in their lives - and that can be empowering for them.

Plus, it can help avoid those power struggles that are so frustrating for both parents and kids!

Giving your child a choice helps them feel like they have some control over their life, which is an important feeling for kids to develop early on. It teaches them how to make decisions and think critically about the options available to them.

When you give them a choice, it shows that you trust them and believe they can make the right decision. It also helps reduce power struggles and arguments between you and your child.

It can also help foster independence in your child. Ultimately, it will help your kid learn how to be a responsible adult.

Some examples of offering your child choices are:

- "Do you want to wear the blue shirt or the green shirt?"
- "Do you want to eat the apple or the orange?"
- "Do you want to watch TV or read a book?"
- "Do you want to go outside and play or stay inside and play?"
- "Do you want to take a bath now or in five minutes?"
- "Should we go on a walk or ride our bikes today?"

Offering choices is a great way to get your kid to listen without having to yell, and it's a good technique to use when you need them to do something they may not want to do.

By giving them options, you are telling them that they have some control over the situation and that their opinion matters. This will make cooperation more likely.

10) Take Breaks

Raising kids is hard. Really hard. And sometimes, when we're feeling overwhelmed, frustrated, and exhausted, it's really tempting to just yell at them to get them to listen.

But yelling is never the answer. Fortunately, there are a few things you can do to get your kid to listen without yelling. One of those things is taking breaks.

Here's how it works: every time you feel yourself getting angry or frustrated, take a break. Step away from your kid for a few minutes, take a deep breath and calm down. You'll be surprised at how much easier it is to deal with them when you're not angry.

Following are a few reasons why breaks are important for your kids as well.

Kids need time to relax and recharge. They're more likely to listen if they're not exhausted.

Breaks help them focus better when they return to tasks. It's a good way to show them that you value their input.

They learn how to take breaks themselves, which is important for their health. It's a good way to connect with your kids and build trust.

Some ways to use breaks effectively are:

- Explain to your child the importance of breaks and why you're taking one
- Set some ground rules for how break time will be used (e.g., no screens, no loud noises)
- Take a break yourself - it's hard to stay calm and focused when you're exhausted
- Make sure your child has a designated place to take breaks (e.g., a special spot in the backyard or a quiet corner of the house)
- Encourage your child to use breaks to relax and recharge,

not just goof off

- Reward your child for following the break rules - even something as simple as an extra five minutes of story time before bed can make a big difference

Taking breaks is important for both kids and adults. It gives us a chance to rest and recharge, which makes it easier to listen and pay attention when we come back.

For parents, this means that taking a break occasionally, can actually help you get your kid's attention without having to yell.

And for kids, it means they can learn better and behave better when they take regular breaks too.

11) Ignore Minor Misbehavior

Kids misbehaving is something parents are all too familiar with. It can be tough to get them to listen but yelling at them usually doesn't work.

Here's another trick that might help - ignore their minor misbehavior. It might sound cruel, but it works! Kids will stop bugging you if they know they won't get any attention for it.

Some reasons why ignoring minor misbehavior works are that ignoring your child's bad behavior will usually make them stop doing it because they want your attention.

It's a way to avoid giving them the satisfaction of seeing you get upset. Kids are more likely to listen when they know their parents are in charge.

You're setting a good example for them by not reacting emotionally to every little thing. It teaches them how to handle frustration and disappointment in life. They'll eventually learn that there are consequences for their actions, even if you don't punish them yourself.

Some examples of ignoring minor misbehavior are:

- Ignore your kid when they're whining or throwing a fit
- Don't give them any attention until they've calmed down and are ready to listen
- Make sure they know that you're only giving them attention when they behave properly
- Explain why it's important to listen and follow directions
- Praise them for good behavior, even if it's just a small act
- Stay consistent with your expectations and rewards/punishments

So, the next time your little one is testing your patience by refusing to put on their shoes, or your preschooler is having a meltdown in the grocery store, take a deep breath and remember that this behavior is all part of their normal development.

And if you can resist the urge to react and instead focus on teaching them how to behave, you'll be setting them up for success both now and in the future.

12) Use Humor

Raising kids is hard. Getting them to listen can be even harder. But what if there was a way to get them to do what you say without having to raise your voice?

Believe it or not, using humor can be another key to success!

So, the next time your little one is testing your patience, try out one of these tips and see how it works for you. You may be surprised at just how well they work!

First, let's look at a few reasons why using humor will help get your little one to listen.

Laughing together is a great way to bond. It shows your kid that you're human and makes them more likely to open-up to you.

Humor can diffuse difficult situations and help kids feel better about themselves.

Laughter distracts from anger or punishment, which can make compliance easier in the future. Kids learn best when they're having fun - humor is a great way to teach them new things.

Some ways you can use humor to get your child to listen are:

- Use humor to get your child's attention
- Make sure your jokes are appropriate for your child's age group
- Be consistent with using humor as a disciplinary tool
- Don't use sarcasm or irony when you're trying to be funny
- Avoid making fun of your child in public
- Laugh along with your child when they tell a joke

If you want to get your kids to listen without having to yell, try using humor. Laughing is a great way to connect with your children and show them that you're on their side. It can also help diffuse tense situations before they get out of hand.

So, the next time Junior decides not to clean his room or Jenny won't stop whining, try cracking a joke instead of raising your voice. You might be surprised at how well it works!

13) Connect with Your Child

Kids can be a handful, especially when they're not listening to what you're saying. But before you put them in time-out or resort to bribery, try connecting with them instead.

According to a study by the University of Missouri, when parents connect with their kids on an emotional level, it leads to better communication and increased obedience.

So, the next time your little one's giving you trouble, take a deep breath and find out what's really going on. You may be surprised at how much easier things will go from there.

Some reasons why connecting with your child to get them to listen are that connecting with your child establishes trust and communication.

It shows them that you care about them and their feelings. It helps them feel safe and secure.

Connecting with your child can prevent behavioral problems later in life. It teaches them how to connect with others. It also strengthens the parent-child bond.

Some examples of connecting with your child to get them to listen are:

- Establish trust by being honest and admitting when you're wrong
- Show them that you care about their feelings and take their opinions into account
- Be a good role model - kids learn more from what we do than what we say
- Set clear boundaries and expectations, and enforce them consistently
- Spend time with your child one-on-one, without distractions
- Listen to them attentively and don't judge or interrupt

Connecting with your child is one of the most important things you can do to help them listen. When children feel connected to their parents, they are more likely to want to please them and follow their directions.

If you're struggling to get your child to listen, try taking a step back and connecting with them on a deeper level. It may be just what they need to start obeying you without having to raise your voice.

14) Be Assertive

Kids have a way of pushing our buttons. No matter how confident we are as parents, there's always one moment where we feel like all our authority is about to fly out the window. In those moments, it's essential that we learn how to be assertive with our kids.

By setting boundaries and sticking to them, we can get them to listen without resorting to yelling or threats.

Some reasons why being assertive is effective, is that when you are assertive, your child knows that you mean business and they are more likely to listen.

Assertiveness shows that you respect yourself and your child, which builds a better relationship. Being assertive sets boundaries for your child so they know what acceptable behavior is and what is not.

When you stand up for yourself, it gives your child permission to do the same in the future. Assertiveness can help prevent power struggles between you and your child.

Firstly, it's important to understand the difference between assertiveness and aggressiveness. Being assertive means standing up for yourself in a calm and confident way. On the other hand, being aggressive means being forceful and demanding.

It's important to be assertive with your children, but not aggressive. If you're too forceful, they'll tune you out and rebel against you. But if you're assertive, they'll understand that you mean business and they're more likely to listen.

Important things to keep in mind when being assertive are:

- Use a calm voice and avoid yelling
- Make sure your child is looking at you when you're speaking to them
- Avoid using threats or ultimatums

- Explain why you want them to do something, rather than just telling them what to do
- Be consistent - if you enforce rules one day but don't the next, your child will be confused

Being assertive with your child is the key to getting them to listen without having to yell. By setting boundaries and communicating expectations concisely, you are teaching them how to behave in a healthy manner both at home and out in the world.

So, the next time your child ignores you or pushes back against your authority, try using some of these techniques for being more assertive.

It may take a little practice, but soon you'll find that they are listening without raising their voice too.

15) Avoid Power Struggles

As a parent, you know that getting your kid to listen can sometimes be challenging. You might find yourself in power struggles with them, trying to get them to do what you want.

But there's a better way. By avoiding power struggles, you can get your kid to listen without resorting to force or threats.

Power struggles can be exhausting and frustrating for both parents and children. They can lead to resentment and anger on both sides.

Children who are used to winning power struggles may have difficulty adjusting to situations where they don't get their way. It's important to set boundaries with your child, but it's also important to find a way to enforce those boundaries without resorting to a power struggle.

There are many ways to achieve this, including using positive reinforcement, establishing rules and consequences, and giving choices whenever possible. By avoiding power struggles, you'll be able to create a more positive and productive relationship with your child.

Some ways you can avoid power struggles are:

- Establish rules and expectations early on
- Explain the consequences of not following the rules
- Be consistent with your discipline techniques
- Stay calm and avoid yelling or getting angry
- Give your child plenty of positive reinforcement when they do follow the rules
- Model good behavior yourself

So, the next time your child is being particularly stubborn, or you feel like a yelling match is imminent, take a step back and try to avoid the power struggle. It might be hard in the moment, but it's worth it in the long run.

Not only will you have a calmer home environment, but your child will also learn how to listen without having to resort to raised voices.

16) Model the Behavior You Want to See

When it comes to getting our kids to listen, actions really do speak louder than words. If you want your kid to clean their room, start by cleaning your own room. If you want them to stop yelling, try not yelling yourself.

It can be tough trying to walk the talk sometimes, but by modelling the behavior we want to see in our kids, we're teaching them what's acceptable and setting a good example for them to follow. And that's definitely worth the effort.

Kids are constantly watching and learning from their parents. If you want your kids to listen, you need to set the example.

Be patient and consistent when teaching your kids how to behave. Reward good behavior and ignore bad behavior (at least in the beginning).

Don't be afraid to get tough if needed - but always be consistent. Take some time for yourself so you can recharge and stay calm.

Some things to keep in mind when trying to get your little one to model your behavior are:

- Model the behavior you want your child to emulate
- Use positive reinforcement when your child does something good
- Explain why you're asking them to do something, and what will happen if they don't listen
- Set rules and expectations that are reasonable and easy to follow
- Stay calm and consistent when dealing with difficult behaviors

- Avoid yelling or spanking - it will only make things worse

If you want to be a good role model for your kid, start by modelling the behavior you want them to exhibit. When they see that you're following through with what you preach, they'll be more likely to listen without having to yell.

And remember, consistency is key – keep up the good work and eventually your child will develop those desirable habits on their own.

17) Use "I" Statements

Do you want your kids to listen to you? It's not as difficult as you may think. Try using "I" statements instead of directives. For example, say "I need you to help me pick up these toys," rather than "Pick up the toys."

Using "I" statements makes it clear that you're asking for help, not issuing an order. Plus, it puts the focus on your needs rather than theirs, which can be a powerful motivator.

Some reasons why "I" statements are effective, are that "I" statements are direct and to the point - your child knows exactly what you want them to do.

"I" statements show that you're taking ownership of your feelings, which can help your child empathize with you. "I" statements are less threatening than other forms of communication, so your child is more likely to listen.

"I" statements help build a positive relationship with your child based on trust and communication. "I" statements can also be used in any situation, whether you're disciplining your child or simply trying to get them to clean their room.

Some tips for using "I" statements effectively are:

- Start with a positive statement

- Explain why you're asking your child to do something
- Use "I" statements to ask your child to do something
- Follow up with a positive statement if your child listens
- Don't get angry or raise your voice if your child doesn't listen - stay calm and try again later

By using "I" statements when you talk to your child, you are teaching them how to listen and understand what someone is saying. Instead of yelling or getting frustrated, they will feel calmer and more willing to hear your point of view.

Try using "I" in your sentence the next time you need to have a serious conversation with your little one – it will make both of your lives easier!

18) Avoid Ultimatums

It's tempting to issue an ultimatum to your child to get them to listen. But before you do, consider the possible consequences. Threatening your child with dire consequences if they don't obey is a surefire way to damage the relationship and foster resentment.

Instead, try using some of the techniques in this book to get your child to comply. With a little patience and perseverance, you can eventually achieve compliance without resorting to threats.

Some of the reasons you should not use ultimatums to get your child to listen are that ultimatums are a way of threatening someone into doing something.

Kids are more likely to rebel against ultimatums. Ultimatums can damage the relationship you have with your child. There are better ways to get your kid to listen that don't involve threats.

Ultimatums should only be used as a last resort.

19) Seek Help from a Professional

If you're still struggling to get your child to listen, it may be time to seek help from a professional. A therapist or counselor can help you identify the root of the problem and come up with a plan to address it.

Don't be afraid to ask for help - there's no shame in admitting that you need assistance. Sometimes all it takes is a fresh perspective to see results.

A therapist or counselor can help you identify the root of the problem and come up with a plan to address it. They also can help you with different techniques to get your kid to listen.

When speaking with a professional, be honest about your concerns and be open to trying new things. With their help, you can get your kid to listen and improve your relationship with them in the process.

Some of the things you can expect are to get help identifying the root of the problem, come up with a plan to address it, and try new techniques.

The benefit of using a professional is that you're more likely to see results due to the fresh perspective.

You know it's time to seek professional help when you're struggling to get your kid to listen, and you've tried the different techniques we've discussed, with no success.

20) Join a Support Group

Do you feel like you're constantly being ignored by your kids? Are they never doing what you ask them to do, no matter how many times you repeat yourself? Join the club! It seems like nowadays kids just don't listen to their parents.

But the good news is that there are plenty of ways to get them to start taking your requests more seriously.

Another great way to do that is by joining a support group for parents. There, you'll be able to share tips and advice with other frustrated parents who are dealing with the same issues as you.

And who knows? You may even find some solutions that work for you.

Some of the reasons a support group can help are that kids are more likely to listen when they know that other people are relying on them.

Joining a support group can also help you find the right techniques to get your kid to listen.

You're not alone - there are plenty of other parents out there who are also struggling with this issue. Support groups can provide a sense of community and support that you may not otherwise have.

Some things that may help when joining a support group are:

- Join a support group to connect with other parents who are going through the same thing
- Show up to meetings prepared with questions and topics for discussion
- Don't be afraid to share your own experiences and advice
- Be an active listener, and don't dominate the conversation
- Follow up with other members after the meeting to continue the discussion

If you're looking for a way to help your kid listen without having to resort to yelling, joining a support group may be the answer. Support groups provide an outlet for parents to share their experiences and learn from others who are in similar situations.

Not only will this help your child develop better listening skills, but it will also show them that it's okay to ask for help when they need it.

HOW TO FORGIVE YOURSELF FOR YELLING AT YOUR CHILD

I f you've ever found yourself yelling at your child, you're not alone. It's a common parenting struggle that many of us face. And it can be hard to forgive ourselves for losing our temper.

But the good news is that it's possible to move past it and continue being the best parent we can be. Here are some tips on how to forgive yourself for yelling at your child:

1) Acknowledge what you did

The first step is to acknowledge what you did. It's important to take responsibility for your actions and understand that what you did was not okay. This will help you move on from the incident and avoid making the same mistake in the future.

2) Understand why you did it

Once you've acknowledged what you did, take some time to understand why you did it. What was going on in your life that led to this? What were the triggers that caused you to lose your temper? Once you know what led to the incident, you can work on avoiding those triggers in the future.

3) Apologize to your child

Once you've taken responsibility for your actions, it's time to apologize to your child. This is an important step in the process of forgiveness. It shows them that you're sorry for what you did and that you're willing to make things right.

4) Plan to avoid it in the future

Now that you know what led to the incident, you can plan to avoid it in the future. This may involve making some changes in your life, such as learning how to better deal with stress. But it's important to do whatever it takes to avoid yelling at your child again.

5) Give yourself some grace

Lastly, give yourself some grace. Parenting is hard, and we all make mistakes. Forgive yourself for what you did and focus on being the best parent you can be from now on.

Nobody's perfect - we all make mistakes. And when we do, it's important to forgive ourselves and move on. These tips will help you do just that.

Last Words From The Book That Will Stop You Yelling At Your Kids

W e've covered the benefits of learning to stop yelling at your little one. We also covered why parents yell and what it accomplishes. As you know, yelling doesn't work in the long run. In fact, it often makes matters worse.

Remember, it's okay to ask for help when you need it. There are plenty of resources out there to help you, including support groups and parenting classes. And if you ever find yourself struggling, just take another look at the tips provided and watch the difference it makes!

If you found that any of the techniques were helpful, please show your appreciation by leaving a review :-)

Printed in Great Britain
by Amazon

16224175R00031